Geoff Boycott on Batting

Also by Geoff Boycott

Geoff Boycott's Book for Young Cricketers

Geoff Boycott on Batting

Stanley Paul
London Melbourne Sydney Auckland Johannesburg

Stanley Paul & Co. Ltd

An imprint of the Hutchinson Publishing Group

3 Fitzroy Square, London W1P 6JD

Hutchinson Group (Australia) Pty Ltd
30–32 Cremorne Street, Richmond South, Victoria 3121
PO Box 151, Broadway, New South Wales 2007

Hutchinson Group (NZ) Ltd
32–34 View Road, PO Box 40–086, Glenfield, Auckland 10

Hutchinson Group (SA) (Pty) Ltd
PO Box 337, Bergvlei 2012, South Africa

First published 1980

Set in Monophoto Times by Tradespools Ltd

Printed in Great Britain by
The Anchor Press Ltd
and bound by Wm Brendon & Son Ltd
both of Tiptree, Essex

British Library Cataloguing in Publication Data
Boycott, Geoff
Geoff Boycott on batting.
1. Cricket – Batting
I. On batting
796.358'26 GV927.5.B3

ISBN 0 09 141770 8 cased
0 09 141771 6 paper

Contents

Acknowledgments

My special thanks to Terry Brindle for the help he has given to me in the preparation of the text, to Bob Drummond and Roy Pell for the instructional photographs, and to Patrick Eagar for all other photographs.

Foreword
by Michael Parkinson

I have been lucky enough to have seen Geoffrey Boycott play in nearly every chapter of his amazing cricketing career. I remember him as a young club player in Yorkshire, full of grit and determination to do well. Then, as now, he never stopped working at his game, never found practising a chore.

I saw him score his first century in a Roses match when he was scarcely razored, an innings which led me to predict that the young Yorkshire opener would not only play for England but would develop into a player comparable with the other great Yorkshire and England opening batsmen, Herbert Sutcliffe and Len Hutton. He has been proving me right ever since.

Geoffrey Boycott is the ideal man to teach cricket. He exemplifies traditional standards, not only of technique but of dress, attitude and behaviour. The young reader would do well to consider *all* these attributes as being important to the game for there is a tendency nowadays to ignore some of them. The point is cricket is a much more enjoyable game to play if you observe all the ground rules.

One final point, Geoffrey Boycott would be the first to admit that he made it to the top not simply because he was a gifted natural player, but more because he worked and worked to make himself a great player.

As a teacher he is the supreme example of someone practising what he preaches – which is practice.

Introduction

When I returned from Australia at the end of the 1978–9 tour I felt in terrible form. I had not played well, and the most common criticisms were that I was using my right hand too much in playing shots and that I was too 'chest on' to the bowler so that most of my strokes were restricted to the leg side.

I had played first-class cricket for sixteen years, played in seventy-nine Test matches and scored over 5000 runs for England, but there was only one place for me before the English season started – back at the nets with my old friend and coach, Johnnie Lawrence, trying to discover what was wrong and get it right again.

We found that I had drifted so far away from the basics that returning to them felt strange for a while. It took me over a month, practising just about every day, to get back to the basic rhythm and technique which I feel is an important part of my game.

The point I am making is that cricket

is not an easy game to master or to play well. I hope this book will help you to develop the basic skills which make playing cricket such a pleasure – but don't expect to become a world beater overnight. Don't become dejected or disillusioned if it takes time to master the basics; remember that it took me a month to get them right after a lapse, and I have played a bit all over the world.

Coaching is very important. I know there is a theory that English players tend to be 'over-coached' but everybody benefits from expert advice, and it is never too early to start. I first went to Johnnie Lawrence's coaching school when I was nine; over the years we have developed a very close relationship and I am never afraid to go back to him when I have a problem with my batting. Listen and learn if you can from someone who has played the game at a high level and really knows what he is talking about.

Practice is most important too, and remember that your mental attitude has to be as right when you are practising as when you are batting. You have to be alert and receptive, and if practice becomes a bore my advice is to give it a rest until you really feel enthusiastic again. Better an hour that you enjoy than a couple of hours just going through the motions.

Having said that, don't kid yourself that you can become a good player without working at it. You have to accept the self-discipline of practice and it is foolish to imagine you can become a decent player just by twirling the bat at weekends. Most professionals have a bat in their hand practically every day during the summer; I know they work at it for a living but if they need the practice to keep in form and improve their game, how much more important for the ambitious young cricketer to use his practice wisely whenever he can.

Cricket is meant to be enjoyed and there are few greater satisfactions than playing any game well. I am often asked which performances have given me most pleasure and that's not an easy one to answer but I suppose among the more recent innings, making a century on my return to Test cricket at Trent Bridge, scoring my hundredth first-class 100 in a Test match at Headingley and making a one-day century against Lillee, Thomson and Walker last winter must rank pretty highly. But there is much satisfaction to be gained from making lower scores on a difficult pitch; it is the knowledge that you have played well which is important.

That being so, just remember that to play consistently well you must master the basics of the game. It's well worth the effort.

1. The grip

The easiest and most natural way to make sure that you are holding the bat properly is to lay it down in front of you and then pick it up as though you were wielding an axe. That way, most of the basic requirements for a correct grip – which is absolutely essential if you are to hit the ball with the full face of the blade on either side of the pitch – will be met quite automatically.

The hands must work together, so they should be close together on the handle. Grip around the middle of the handle – better nearer the top than the bottom but modern bats are balanced to be held in the middle – and hold the handle firmly. A lot of youngsters make the mistake of simply cushioning the bat in the palm of their hands and this leads to bad habits, as we will see later. If it seems difficult to grip the bat comfortably it is probably because the handle is too thick; professionals tend to have quite large and strong hands so they can tackle a thicker handle; it is

Leg Glance Off the Backfoot

Attacking Off the Backfoot

Playing Forward Defensively

Moving Out to Drive

important to make sure that your hands can close round the bat handle comfortably.

If you use the 'axeman' technique, the *V*s formed by the first finger and thumb of each hand are on the same line halfway between the outside edge and the splice (Photo 1). That's fine. When you face a bowler, the back of your left hand faces towards mid-off or extra cover.

1

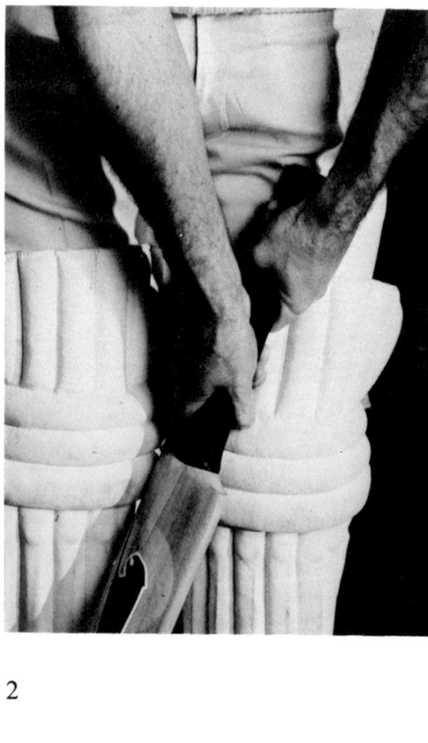

2

The function of the hands is vitally important; it cannot be stressed too often that the left hand controls the whole stroke. The left hand should be firm but flexible, and not rigid, and it should not move once you have positioned it correctly on the handle.

The right hand is basically a steadying influence, but it is also the hand which exerts power into the stroke. That being so, a lot of batsmen tend to allow it to dominate – a perfectly natural temptation since most batsmen are right-handed. But you must guard against the right hand dominating because it will lead to power without control; the right hand takes over and drags the ball to the on-side.

Perhaps one reason for this is that correct use of the left hand, especially in beginners, tends to produce some strain and tension in the left wrist. Youngsters especially complain that the left wrist begins to ache, so they tend to let the right take over. Persevere and, if it helps, use a fairly solid object such as a squash ball to help strengthen the left wrist. Squeeze it firmly, hold it for a few seconds, relax and then repeat the cycle. You can do that without any inconvenience while you are waiting to bat – or even at home reading a book or watching TV! I have used a squash ball

in this way for years and it certainly helps.

One of the commonest faults is to grip the handle with the hands apart. It feels OK but the hands automatically work against each other when a batsman tries to play properly . . . the right hand inevitably takes over and the batsman develops a scything action. Proper positioning and the correct tension in the grip – firm but not rigid – avoid that pitfall.

Some players do hold their hands apart on the handle. I suppose an obvious example is Asif Iqbal, whose 'open-handed' grip is very noticeable because he uses a long-handled bat. Asif is a world-class batsman, so clearly that form of grip works for him. But the grip with hands together is the best for the vast majority of players and in any case, the right hand must not be allowed to dominate; Asif still fashions his shots using his left shoulder and elbow; he does not allow his right hand to take over.

Naturally, there are exceptions to every rule, and there is room for modification in the basic grip. Let me stress that the grip I have outlined is the best for any batsman to develop; it is the one which the vast majority of players should be able to master and use effec-

2

tively. But there *are* individual differences and the chief one probably involves turning the left hand slightly further round the handle (Photo 2), I tend to do this and so did Sir Leonard Hutton, so it cannot be entirely ineffective. If a more rounded grip with the *V* of the left hand pointing down the splice of the bat comes more naturally, then use it – it's a 'good fault', because it gives

extra control, especially on difficult pitches. Some claim it limits driving power because of the extra strain on the left wrist but it didn't exactly do Hutton a lot of harm!

2. The stance

Cricketers come in all shapes and sizes, so it is inevitable that there are apparent differences in the stances of players, even of experienced professionals, at the crease. But the basics of the stance are the same . . . the aims are comfort, balance and mobility.

Feet should be placed comfortably, about 6 to 8 inches apart, on either side of the popping crease, with the weight distributed evenly for mobility (Photos 3 and 4). Never put your weight on your heels, but bend the knees slightly until you feel poised enough to play back or forward.

Players generally find it most comfortable to ground the bat just behind the toes of their right foot and rest the hands lightly on their left thigh. And that being so, it is important to choose the right size of bat: one which is too big – a common fault among youngsters who reckon they will buy a big bat and 'grow into it' – makes a comfortable stance impossible.

3

4

If the bat is too big, one of two obvious faults will develop. Either the batsman rests it naturally on his left thigh and then has to ground it well behind his feet. Or he tucks it into his boot and finds the handle poking somewhere into his stomach. Either way, he is in trouble before he starts.

Cricket is a sideways game as far as throwing, bowling and batting are concerned and it is vital that a batsman adopts a sideways stance. If the feet are roughly parallel with the popping crease, the body will face approximately towards point and at 90 degrees to the bowler. That is the best position.

What makes it hard for many inexperienced batsmen is that they become tense, over-determined and they stoop . . . and that is the worst possible fault in the stance. When a batsman stoops he immediately drags his head down, which makes it impossible to level his eyes correctly.

The head must always be kept still and the eyes must be on the same level, otherwise they cannot focus properly.

Some players – Greg Chappell and myself, for instance – move the right foot slightly back and across when the bowler is two or three strides from his delivery. This brings the head a little more over to the off-side, but the weight

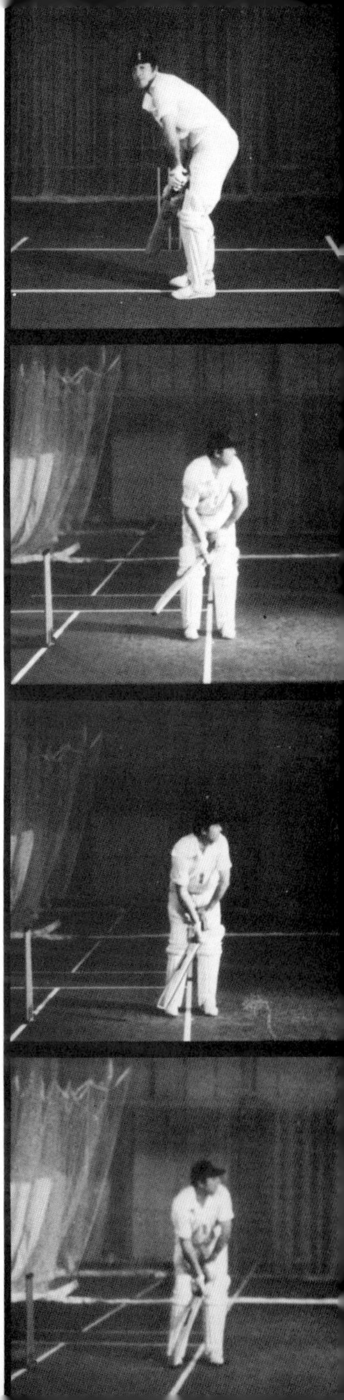

is still on both feet, balanced and poised to move back or forward depending on the stroke to be played. The vitally important thing is that as the ball is delivered, the head is absolutely still.

I first started this slight movement of the right foot in 1964 when I found Australia's Graham Corling was getting me out rather too regularly. I was edging deliveries without really knowing why and I had to do something about it. With this new method I found that I had a better idea of the position of my off stump, so I have used a back-and-across movement ever since – but let me stress again that the head must be still when the ball is delivered.

3. The two-shouldered stance

You often hear players and spectators talk about a 'two-eyed stance' when in fact every stance in cricket involves the use of both eyes. Poor Colin Milburn lost the sight of one eye and consequently found it impossible to continue in the game.

What people really mean is a two-shouldered stance (Photo 5); although it is not recommended as a basic method it can have its uses for the batsman who finds constant difficulty in playing deliveries pitched on his legs.

No leading player uses the two-shouldered stance regularly at the moment, but it worked well enough for Jim Parks and Ken Barrington in the past. The important thing is to learn the correct stance first and then use this more chest-on stance for tactical reasons.

From a normal 'sideways' stance the batsman simply opens his feet and shoulders so that he is more chest-on to the bowler. I used this stance quite a

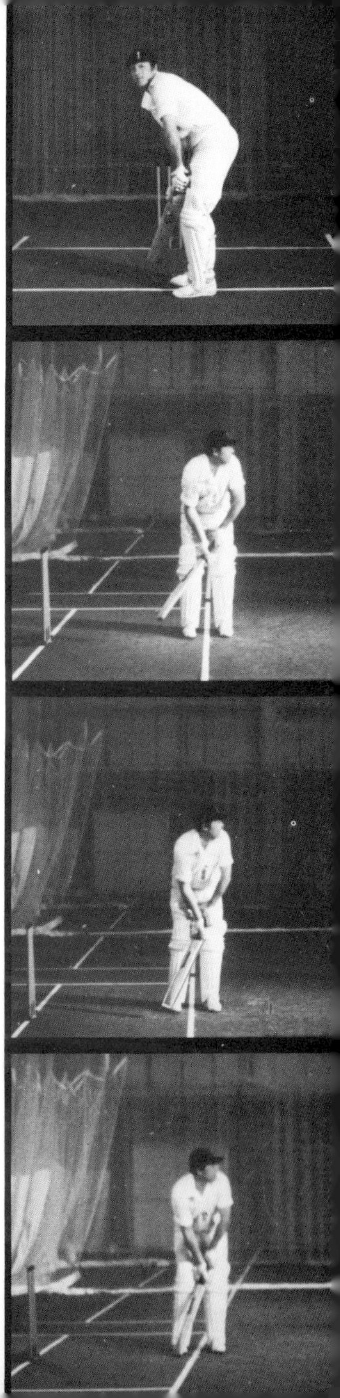

5

bit in Australia in 1978/9 because I was troubled by an old thumb injury and found it impossible to grip comfortably with my left hand.

An open stance obviously helps a batsman play on the leg side because his body is already turned; he finds it easier to on-drive, hook and pull. But equally, strokes on the off-side are restricted because the left foot and body have a long way to come round, and most batsmen find this very inhibiting.

The natural arc of the bat from a two-shouldered stance tends to be from inside to out, which is risky in itself.

4. The backlift

The backlift is far more important to good stroke-play than many young batsmen realize. The straighter the backlift, the better the chance of playing the ball with a straight bat – but like everything else a proper backlift needs to be learned and practised.

Contrary to what you might expect, the left arm and wrist, not the right hand, do nearly all the work. The head and body should be kept quite still and the bat is taken back by the left hand (Photo 6); the face of the bat opens quite naturally towards point as the bat lifts.

Practise taking the bat up straight in front of a mirror. It is not a natural action, it requires effort and persistence and young players often complain that the left shoulder, arm and wrist begin to ache, but don't weaken. Once you have learned to pick up the bat straight, you will find that it is much easier to swing straight and therefore play the ball with a straight bat.

6

There is an excellent way of practising that, too. Drill a hole in a composition ball, fix it to a length of wire (string will break), then fasten it to a beam or tree so that the ball hangs just below waist height. Now concentrate on swinging through the ball – smoothly not violently – with a straight bat. If you make correct contact the ball will swing back to its original position for you to hit it

again and again; if you hit it at an angle the ball will fly off at an angle and you will know that you need more practice. A very simple exercise but one which I have found most useful – after all, most cricket shots are played with a vertical movement of the bat, so here is a fundamental which simply cannot be practised too much.

One point of explanation. The back-lift-in-the-mirror exercise will probably show that the bat is rarely lifted perfectly straight; it is bound to wander slightly 'off line' but you need not worry – provided it comes down straight. That is absolutely vital, and although many players in the first-class game do not pick up perfectly straight the good batsmen always come down straight. The greatest of them all, Sir Donald Bradman, used to pick up his bat in the direction of gulley! But it looped at the top and invariably came down straight; I don't think Sir Don missed too many. . . .

Spectacles can be a bit of a nuisance to a batsman and I find contact lenses much easier to get along with. But if a keen batsman does wear glasses I recommend rimless ones if possible, or at least glasses with light alloy frames. They should fit snugly across the bridge of the nose and behind the ears: few things destroy concentration quicker than squinting past a solid spectacle frame or wondering just when the spectacles themselves are likely to fall off.

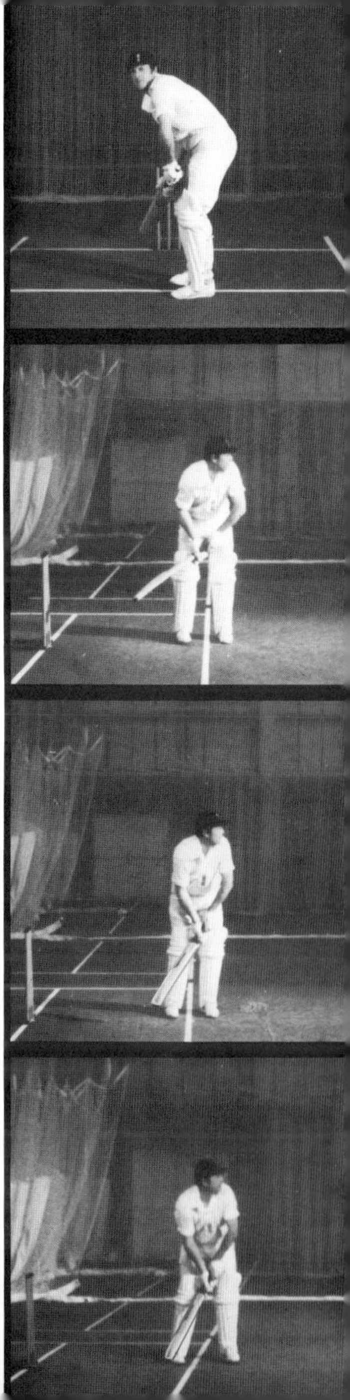

5. Taking guard

It is worth pausing for a moment to consider the business of taking guard – if only because most batsmen outside the professional game have little clear idea why they take guard at all! They sing out 'middle' or 'two legs' quite happily without really stopping to consider why they do it. Most of them probably reckon it gives them room for a favourite shot.

Batsmen take guard because they need to know exactly where their stumps are and – most important of all – where their off stump is. That is the great danger area. The best way to sort out a guard to suit you best is to adopt your normal stance and then ask a friend, standing where the umpire stands, to move you along until your eyes are just over the off stump. That's your guard.

By the way, I know many club cricketers ask for a guard 'from where the bowler bowls'. That makes no sense at all. Take your guard from over and behind the bowler's wicket; after all, that's where the umpire will be when he gives you out (or not out) l.b.w. . . .

So far we have concentrated on the preparation for batting, on the basic principles which are bound to dictate your method and, perhaps, how successfully you play. But cricket is a mobile game played against a ball which arrives at varying speeds and heights, always likely to deviate. A batsman with both feet set in tubs of concrete hasn't a chance.

Good footwork is vital. The link between eyes, brain and feet enables a batsman to decide how he intends to play a delivery and then to position himself quickly but without being hurried or forced off balance.

The best players in the modern game can play off front or back foot. Less gifted players tend to play on the front foot in defence or attack because playing off the back foot is harder. 'When in doubt, push out' is a fair maxim in most circumstances; it is certainly safe if only because umpires are less likely to give l.b.w. decisions against a batsman pushing well forward.

But the player who goes on the front foot to virtually every delivery is restricting himself unnecessarily. He can-

not hook, cut or pull, his range of shots is severely limited and he is immediately handing the bowler an advantage he has not earned.

Every batsman has his favourite strokes and plays some shots better than others. But it is foolish to restrict yourself as a matter of policy; think in terms of playing forward or back and treat every delivery strictly on its merits.

6. Playing forward defensively

The forward stroke is one of the most important in cricket. Not only does it enable a batsman to survive against good deliveries but it forms the basis of all the drives. Learn to play it correctly and you are half-way to becoming a good batsman.

The object is to play the ball as close as possible to where it pitches, so there must be a determined forward movement with the left leg (Photos 7 and 8). Lead towards the ball with the left shoulder and head, move the left foot to the pitch of the ball and let the weight of your body come forward until the left knee bends slightly.

Lift the heel of the right foot off the ground and tip the body forward – most important, since at the moment of impact the head and eyes should virtually be over the ball, looking down and watching it on to the bat.

The most common fault associated with this stroke is that batsmen do not get on to the toe of the right foot – so

7

8

the left knee is not bent enough, the head is not tipped over the ball, and the batsman simply stands up and pushes the ball away from his body.

Similarly, many batsmen do not take a big enough step with the left foot – the head is left behind and the ball is played with a huge gap between bat and body. It is imperative to play the ball close to the pad to 'shut the gate'. Remember also that the further away you are from the pitch of the ball, the more time it has to seam or perhaps turn and take the edge of the bat.

Get well forward; bend the left knee; get on to the toe of the right foot. These are the three basic principles which must be observed.

The grip of the hands on the bat is also vital. Again, the left hand controls the stroke and the right hand assumes a secondary, guiding function. In the forward defensive stroke these roles are very pronounced.

The left hand keeps the handle in front of the blade, and the right hand relaxes its grip into one between thumb and first two fingers. It is impossible to play the shot correctly if the bat is gripped in the palm of the right hand. In fact as the left hand pushes down and forward, the right tends to pull the blade back.

That means that, when contact is made, the bat is angled sharply down and the ball is smothered. The ball is met with the full face of the bat, but there is no follow-through because the object is simply to kill the ball, not to force it away.

One point which may seem obvious but is often overlooked: if a batsman is playing a defensive stroke there is no sense at all in playing at deliveries he can leave alone. One of the secrets of good batsmanship – and it applies particularly to opening batsmen because they face a fresh attack and a new ball always likely to deviate – is judging which ball to play and which not to play. There is nothing more frustrating for a bowler than to see a batsman judge perfectly when he must defend his wicket and when he can safely let the ball go through.

When you are playing defensively, play decisively or leave the ball alone; do not fence with deliveries outside the off stump.

The forward defensive stroke to a delivery pitching on or about the leg stump is a difficult shot which takes a considerable amount of practice. The first and most important movement is to dip the left shoulder, forcing the head to follow. Then it is vital that the left foot is put across to land just *outside* the line of the ball, with the toe pointing straight down the pitch.

It sounds relatively straightforward but the forward defensive is a difficult stroke to master and needs a lot of hard work. Few young players take to it naturally because they find it hard to balance; they tend to position their feet badly, try to swat at the ball from round the pad and find themselves playing across the line or falling over.

One very good practice for all the forward defensive shots involves four players on any hard and flat surface. Draw a target on the ground about 6 inches deep and 20 inches across on to which the bowler, standing 7 or 8 yards away, lobs the ball underarm.

The batsman positions himself so that he can play forward defensively, and two fielders stand at short mid-on and short mid-off. Straight balls should be played straight back and others on the appropriate line on either side of the pitch. Three or four minutes with the bat each, then change round; it is a very useful exercise.

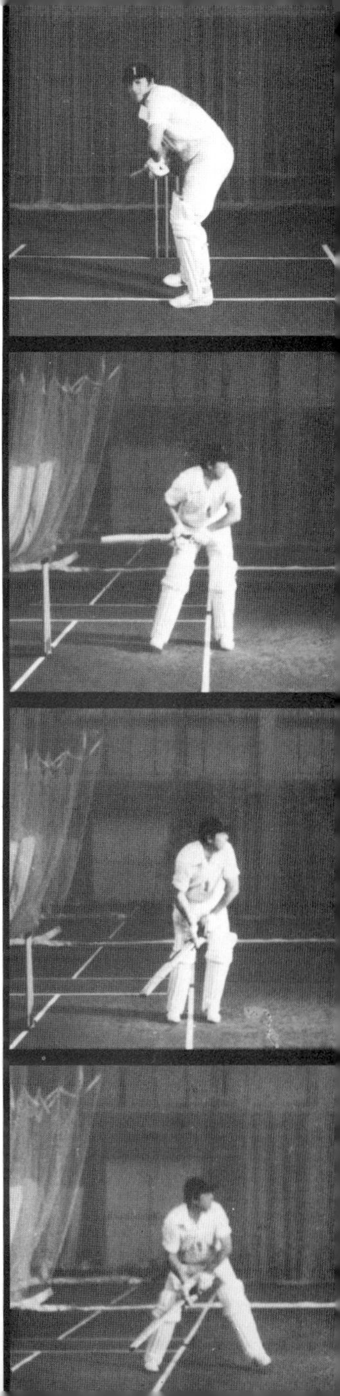

7. Driving off the front foot

Every batsman's natural inclination is to attack the ball, and the drive is the most satisfying stroke in the game. The technique of driving is really the same as for the forward defensive strokes, except that the bat is lifted higher and the ball is met beside the left foot rather than in front of it.

Power for driving comes from creating a bigger pendulum with the bat, a long, smooth swing which takes the bat *through* the ball rather than to the ball. It is controlled throughout by the left arm and hand; the right hand gives steadiness and extra punch at the moment of impact but it is important that the right hand does not come into the shot too soon. If it does, it will drag the bat across the line of the ball.

As in the forward defensive stroke, lead with the head, left shoulder and hip on to the line of the over-pitched ball. For the on-drive turn and dip your shoulder towards mid-on and strike the ball *inside* the big toe of your front (left)

Sunil Gavaskar, one of the finest batsmen India has produced in recent years, drives classically through the covers. His head and body are perfectly balanced.

foot, which should be taking your weight.

For the off-drive, the left shoulder turns and points towards extra cover (Photos 9 and 10). The head is kept

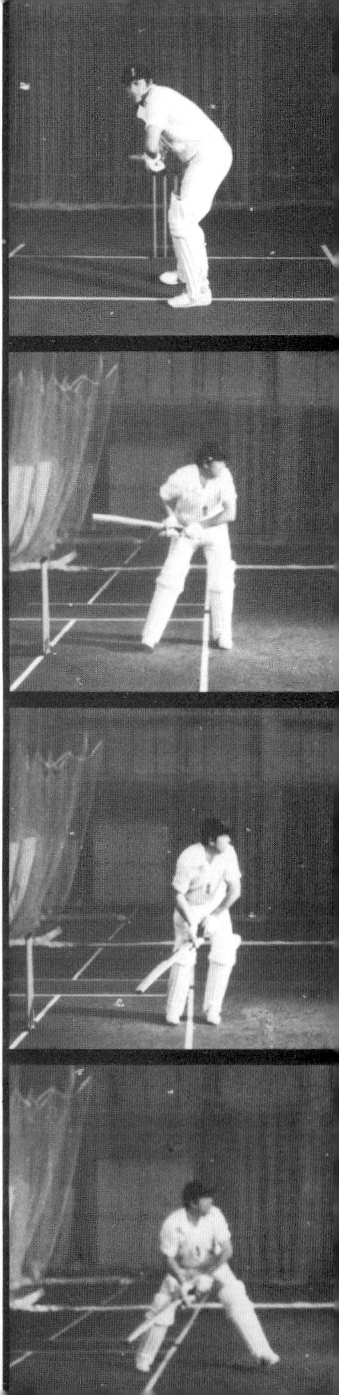

close to the left shoulder so that the eyes look down on the line of the ball. The wider the delivery, the more you turn your back on the bowler. That ensures you stay sideways on and get your left foot to the pitch of the ball.

The movement of the right foot varies, according to whether the drive is on the off-side, straight, or to leg. For

9

10

the off and straight drives (Photos 11 and 12), keep the inside of the right foot on the ground after the shot. The right heel naturally eases, allowing weight to be transferred to the left foot, but the right foot remains steady – not anchored to the ground but providing a balancing point and a base for the shot.

11

12

Strong all around the wicket, Australia's captain Greg Chappell is seen here driving through the on-side.

When driving on the on-side (Photos 13, 14 and 15), don't leave the right foot behind. It is natural and comfortable for the right foot to follow through

13

14

15

with the stroke; in fact it is almost impossible to drive properly on the on-side if the right foot is left in the crease.

It is important to watch the ball all the way on to the bat. That may seem obvious but it does mean that you have to keep your head still and avoid the temptation to lift your eyes and follow the ball. Golfers who do that usually

come to grief and the ball *they* are trying to hit keeps obligingly still!

Think in terms of hitting the ball firmly and cleanly rather than belting the cover off it. If you strain for power you will lose your rhythm without gaining much effect; proper timing and co-ordination will produce a powerful stroke.

Provided the stroke is played correctly, the follow-through is really a matter of what feels most comfortable. Some batsmen, like Ian Botham and Clive Lloyd, have a full, even extravagant follow-through which takes the bat right over the left shoulder; I tend to bend the left elbow and cut my follow-through rather shorter.

A shorter follow-through is often developed by batsmen who face difficult pitches early in their career and opt for control at the expense of a little power. But it does not significantly affect the stroke, provided everything else is right, so it is a matter of personal preference.

8. Moving out to drive

We have already discussed the importance of footwork in batting. This is most evident when a batsman uses his feet against a slow, well-flighted delivery, moving down the pitch to prevent a bowler from dropping unchallenged on to a nagging length. The alert batsman does not allow himself to be dictated to and always looks for an opportunity to get down the pitch.

A simple left-right-left movement of the feet should be enough to create a position where the ball has become a half volley. The bat is lifted high, the weight is pushed forward on to the left foot, the left shoulder faces the bowler, then the right foot glides smoothly up to and behind the left foot, head and left shoulder still leading; finally the left leg goes to the pitch of the ball and the drive is completed with the body weight on the left foot to provide a firm base.

The decision when to go down the

pitch is a matter of judgement and experience but you should be looking for the opportunity to do so when every ball is bowled. Don't go too soon – certainly not before the ball has left the bowler's hand – or he will see your intention and alter his pace or length to beat you. Don't go too late, or you will not get to the pitch of the ball.

By the time you have completed your left–right–left foot movement you should be in position to drive the ball just as if you were playing from the crease. And left–right–left should be enough; if it is necessary to take any more paces it is likely that the delivery was so short it should have been played off the back foot.

Practice, as ever, is essential and I have found two useful ways of practising the drives. For the on- and off-drives, the bowler stands some $2\frac{1}{2}$ feet in front and to the off-side of the batsman, so that the ball dropped from his outstretched hand falls just in front of the batsman's left foot. The batsman drives the ball on the half volley of its second bounce.

Practice for moving out to drive is the same, except that the bowler stands some 4 or 5 feet in front and to the off-side of the batsman, again dropping the ball from a height. The batsman once more moves out and drives the ball on the half volley of its second bounce.

9. Playing back defensively

The ability to play forward is the essence, the most vital part of batting, but if it is coupled with a sound back-foot game it produces a more complete, versatile player who is so much more difficult to defeat. In present-day cricket at the highest level the ability to play off the back foot is essential because there are so many quick bowlers around.

The stroke is easily played once the batsman has persuaded himself to get in line. Most young batsmen have a natural tendency to step away from the ball, because they are nervous of the short-pitched delivery and because they want to give themselves room to hit at it. But we are talking about playing a short delivery with safety, so it is important to get into line.

The right foot moves well back and just inside the line of the ball with the toe pointing parallel to the crease (Photos 16 and 17). Make a conscious effort to step back, don't just shuffle; surprisingly enough the positive action

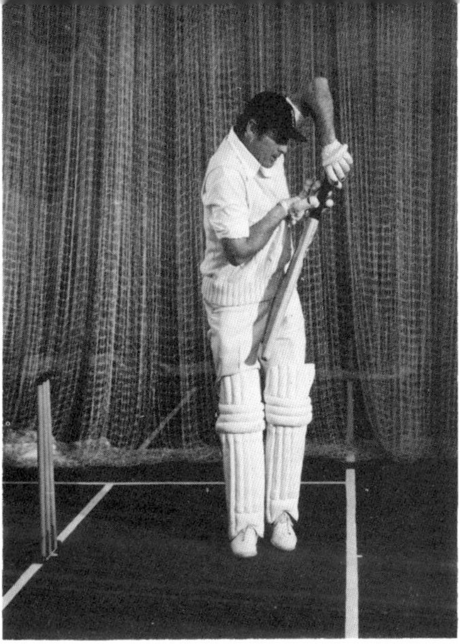

16

17

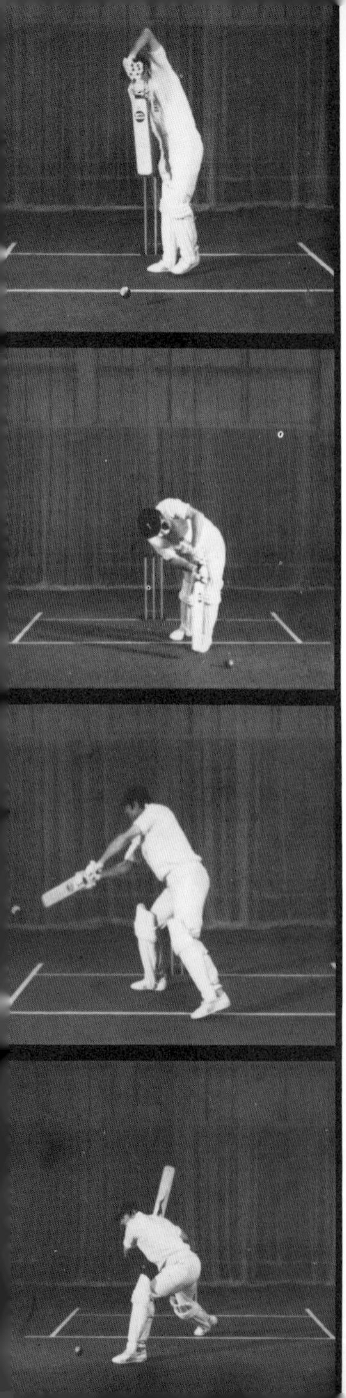

of stepping back helps you relax. And make sure the right foot is kept parallel to the crease; that ensures you keep sideways on to the ball.

The weight is transferred on to the ball of the right foot, and the left foot acts as a balancer. It is a fundamental mistake to stamp the right foot down flat because mobility is important – after all, you are playing the stroke against a fast, rising delivery.

Keep the left elbow high. That makes it easy to control the bat while allowing the right hand to relax into a thumb-and-finger grip; I personally allow the right hand to slide down until it is touching the shoulder of the bat as I feel it gives me even more control.

Now let the ball come on to the bat, meeting it just below the eyes, which should be as level as possible. Don't poke forward at the ball; there is no point in playing back and then going to meet it with the bat held miles away from the body. Keep the head slightly forward and let the ball come on to a dead bat.

Playing a delivery aimed at the body requires a slightly different technique. The natural inclination is to move to the leg side and play the delivery as if it were a straightish ball on the off – but again, it is important to get into line.

The only difference between this and the back-foot defensive stroke is that the right foot need not be parallel to the crease. Turn the right foot until it points towards cover, which automatically turns the body more 'chest-on' to the bowler and gives you room to use the bat. If you do not turn your body you will feel tucked up and cramped.

10. Attacking off the back foot

This is a most difficult stroke for any young player – there are many experienced batsmen who cannot play it well. The shot requires height and strength in the forearms and wrists, and most young players, naturally, have neither.

The bat is lifted high and the body must be kept sideways (Photos 18 and 19). The batsman stands up straight and on his toes to get as much height as he can. The left arm again controls the stroke with the left elbow kept high, though the right hand is used to add punch to the shot just before impact. The right hand grips not with the palm, but with the thumb and fingers.

It is a compact shot with a short hitting area, and the bat is kept on the line of the ball for a short distance after impact before the wrists 'break' naturally.

As I have said, the stroke places a lot of strain on wrists and forearm and many youngsters become frustrated and

18

19

prefer to step away and slog at the ball. But it really is worth practising and any ambitious young batsman should learn to play it the right way – with a straight bat – even if at first he finds it hard to force the ball away. That extra height and strength will come.

So far we have dealt chiefly with those strokes which require a straight bat and therefore a considerable amount of technique and practice. A young player will never become a good batsman unless he learns to play straight but he must also learn to punish the bad ball – and this is often achieved with a cross-bat, horizontal stroke.

Cross-bat strokes come naturally to young players. The right hand dominates; the strokes fulfil the young batsman's natural desire to whack the ball hard. But you only have to look at how often batsmen get out playing cross-bat strokes to realize that they, too, need care and practice; they need to be played properly rather than just energetically.

11. The pull and the hook

We can discuss these shots together because the basic footwork and positioning is virtually the same for both. Play them against any short delivery coming at the body or on a line just outside the off stump – but, if the delivery is wider than that, either leave it or cut, don't try to drag the ball across.

Footwork in both strokes is absolutely vital; the most common fault among young batsmen is not moving their feet decisively and quickly into position; they paddle at the ball with their arms. Good pullers and hookers begin with footwork.

The right foot is taken well back, pointing down the pitch to open the body. It goes outside the line of the ball, so that for the pull the head is in line with the ball and for the hook it is just inside the line (Photos 20 and 21). Again, resist the common fault not to get far enough over and don't plant your feet flat-footed; the weight should always be on the balls of the feet.

20

21

Vivian Richards looks almost casual as, in ideal position, he hooks a short ball through square-leg.

With the weight on the right foot, the left leg is carried away to open the body further and the ball is met with the arms at full stretch – but comfortably extended, not rigid or tense. Don't let

the ball come close to the body, as that stifles and cramps the stroke.

The right hand dominates naturally, and to play the shots with an element of safety it is necessary to roll the right hand over the left at the moment of impact. This turns the blade of the bat downwards and – hopefully – prevents the ball from being skied (Photos 22 and 23).

22

23

Although the foot movement is a backward one, the balance of head and body remains forward; the emphasis is on speed of positioning and timing rather than on effort in hitting. Keep your eye on the ball, especially when hooking; the alternative can be very painful.

A special word about the hook. It can only be played to a delivery arriving

chest high or above. If the ball gets very high, and reaches a point where you are no longer in control of the shot let it pass; otherwise you are just swiping at it. There is more risk to this shot than most, so you must be in control. It requires great speed of movement to be played successfully, and there is an obvious element of physical risk involved in standing up to short-pitched bowling. For these reasons many coaches advise young players never to hook. I can't agree with them. I was eleven years old when I misjudged a hook and went off to hospital to have four stitches put in a gash above my right eye, and I still have the scar. So I am not a compulsive hooker, but I believe it is a stroke which should be mastered and played with discretion.

Cricket is a bit like chess; there are only so many pieces and a good player makes use of them all. Cutting out the hook as a matter of principle surrenders a potential advantage to the bowler and wastes one of the most exhilarating shots in the game.

The point is that the hook, with its in-built element of physical danger, must be played properly – and that means with very quick footwork – and it must be played selectively. Provided a batsman picks his time and place and weighs up all the circumstances, the hook is as legitimate a stroke as the forward defensive. Those circumstances, incidentally, must include such factors as the condition of the pitch, the pace of the bowling, the batsman's personal form, and whether the ball is new or old. But in the end it is a personal decision which only the batsman can make.

Learn to play the hook but, most important, learn to play it well. And that means very quick footwork, taking the right foot over and well back to put as much time and distance between yourself and the pitch of the ball as possible. Every fraction of a second helps. It also means positioning your head outside the line of the ball so that if you fail to connect the ball does not connect with you! And if you get outside the line and then decide against the shot, you can fall away and avoid the ball quite naturally.

12. Hitting a full toss . . .

. . . is a good deal more difficult than it sounds, or than most spectators seem to appreciate. They imagine that any full toss is a cheap and easy way for a batsman to make runs – but look how many times batsmen get out to a full toss.

That is chiefly because a high full toss is a very difficult delivery to hit safely. It is virtually impossible to get on top of the ball and keep it down so I advise a batsman faced with a chest-high full toss to play a straight bat and defend.

If the delivery arrives below chest height it can be attacked – but again a proper approach is most important, and the batsman should curb his desire to belt it out of the ground. Many youngsters get out to a full toss because they let the ball come on too close to them and then try to hit it with their arms bent. The cardinal rule is to take the ball early, on the front foot if possible and with the arms at full stretch (Photos 24 and 25). And always, al-

24

25

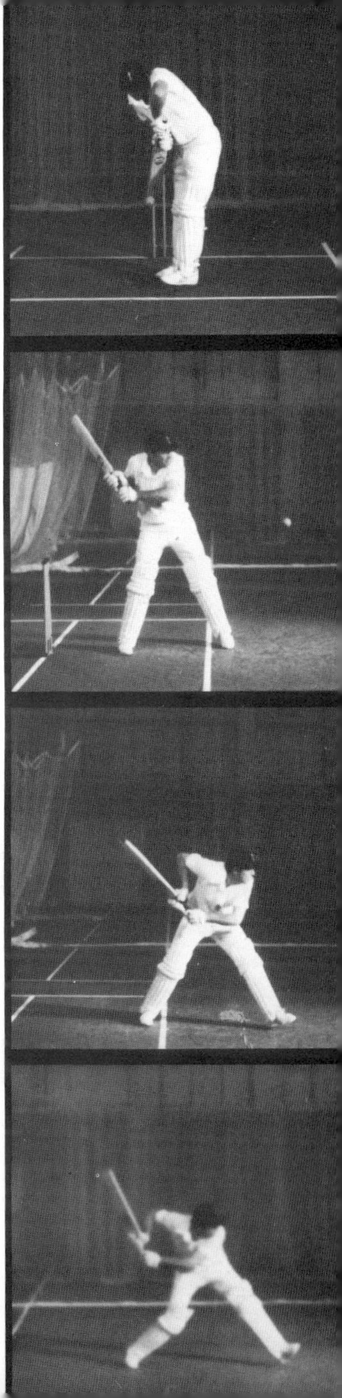

ways, keep your eye on the ball. The ability to hit a full toss properly is particularly useful to young batsmen because, with the greatest respect to young bowlers, they are likely to meet more full tosses at that age than later in their career.

13. The sweep

As its name suggests, the sweep shot is a controlled, flowing movement rather than a violent one. The aim is to help the ball firmly on its way rather than launch a fierce attack. But it is a very effective stroke, when properly played, and can disrupt any spin bowler's field, especially because you will be hitting into the arc behind square leg where the bowler is allowed only two fielders.

When sweeping the well-pitched-up delivery outside the leg stump, the left foot must be positioned inside the line of the ball. Then if you miss with the shot, your wicket is protected by your left pad; since the ball has pitched outside the leg stump you cannot be out l.b.w.

Bend the right leg to drop your body close to the ground, and swing down and through the ball (Photos 26 and 27), not at it. If you simply strike at the ball and it bounces or deviates the chances are that you will get a top edge, so swing smoothly through the ball,

26

27

again with arms well extended. Sweep it, don't smash it.

Use the sweep shot only when the ball pitches outside the leg stump or when the pitch is so difficult that it is hard to drive with safety. It has become increasingly fashionable – perhaps because of the influence of limited-overs cricket where improvisation is important – to sweep the ball off the stumps. But I believe that if a delivery pitches on the line of the stumps it should be driven with a straight bat.

An over-pitched delivery on the line of leg and middle stumps is ripe for the on-drive and a batsman who sweeps instead is using an inferior stroke. The sweep is an alternative stroke to the drive, but a lesser alternative.

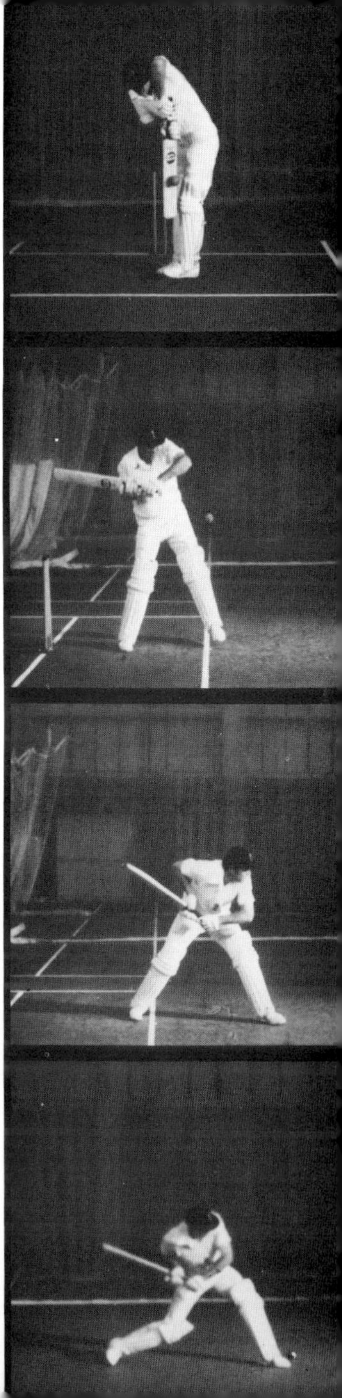

14. The cut

Young players receive a fair number of deliveries wide of the stumps so the cut is a very useful weapon for making runs. It can be employed against any delivery which is short and wide of the off stump, particularly from a quick bowler.

Width and length are important. The ball must be short enough to allow the batsman to watch it rise off the pitch and wide enough to give him room for the stroke. If the delivery is not all that wide, use the back-foot forcing shot (page 42) instead.

The square cut involves two straightforward movements: correct use of the feet, then a down-and-out stroke with the bat coming from as high as possible.

It is basically a one-footed shot. Take the right foot well back and across the stumps with the toes facing towards point to keep you sideways on. The weight is transferred firmly to the right foot and the bat is lifted high (Photo 28); coming down on the ball reduces the

28

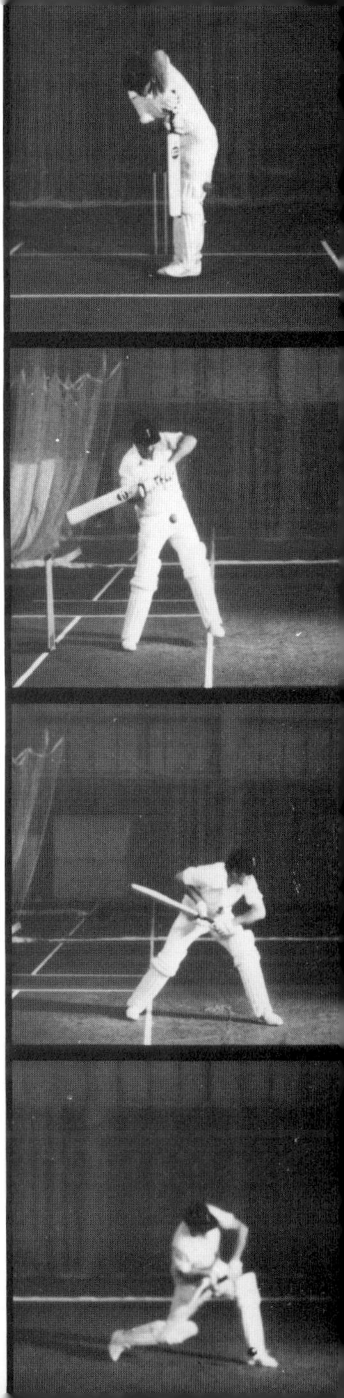

risk of getting an edge if it bounces a little more than expected.

Stand as tall as you can and fling the bat downwards and outwards, coming on to the ball from above; then bend the right knee slightly to allow the body to come into the stroke (Photos 29 and 30). Again – correct positioning of the feet is the basis of the stroke and a high backlift is vital to make it effective.

29

30

15. The late cut

This delicate refinement of the square cut aims at guiding the ball fine behind the stumps on the off-side. That being so,

31

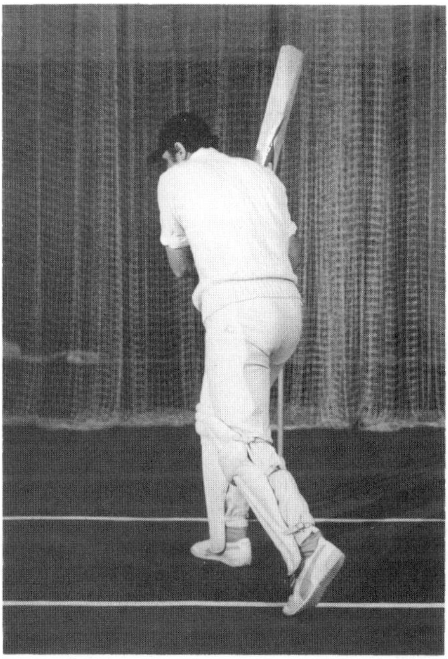

the left shoulder must come round to the point where the bowler is looking at the batsman's back and left shoulder-blade.

To achieve that the right foot is taken not just across, but back and across, with the toes pointing towards third man. There is a pronounced turn of the left shoulder and the bat is lifted high to give plenty of room (Photo 31).

32

33

Let the ball go past your body so that it is level with the stumps, then caress it away using the pace of the ball to add impetus to the stroke (Photos 32 and 33). Played at its best it is a very delicate shot; Alan Knott is one of the best late-cutters in the game, and he takes the ball very late as do all the best exponents of this shot.

Sometimes it is best to forego the

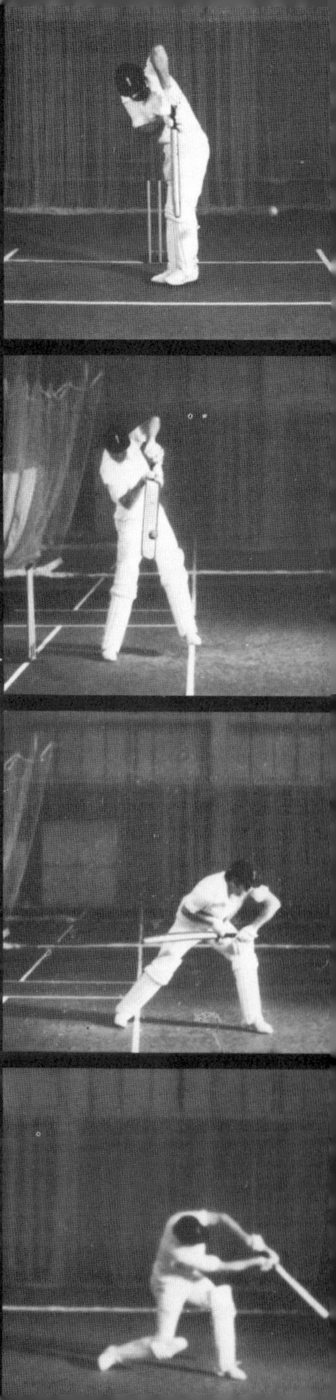

late cut on a slow pitch because there is not enough pace in the ball to make it an effective shot. It is a stroke most often used on firm surfaces.

16. Leg glances

These deflections of the ball can be used when a batsman is having difficulty forcing the ball through the on side. Against quick bowling the ability to glance the ball off the side or hip is very useful – but it is not a substitute for on-driving or any of the more positive shots. Never think in terms of glancing for a single when you might play a positive stroke with the chance of more runs.

Having said that, the leg glance can, by force of necessity, become a very valuable means of keeping the score moving along when the bowling rules out other forms of attack.

Remember that the glance is played with the full face of a vertical bat (Photo 34). Let the ball come on and at the moment of impact close the face of the bat slightly – take care not to turn the face of the bat too soon or you run the risk of meeting the ball with a leading edge. Play the ball just in front of the left pad.

Viv Richards again, this time proving that he can be as delicate as he is devastating, gliding his leg-glance away and simultaneously setting off for a run.

On the front foot, position the left leg inside the line of the ball so that even if you miss completely it will pass harmlessly down the leg side. Because

34

you are playing the ball to leg there is a tendency to use the right arm to steer the ball – resist it and keep the left elbow well up to dictate the shot. Elbow well up, left hand in control, head well over the ball.

Played off the back foot, the stroke is similar to the back defensive (Photos 35 and 36). It is essential to open the body a little and turn towards the ball,

35

36

so the right leg is taken well back and across the stumps with the toes pointing towards mid-off or cover. Bring the left leg close to the right, stand as tall as possible and play the ball off the left pad or hip with the head over the point of impact. Again, the left elbow is carried high and the left hand is in control, slightly closing the face of the bat to deflect the ball to fine leg. Let the ball come well on before you play it.

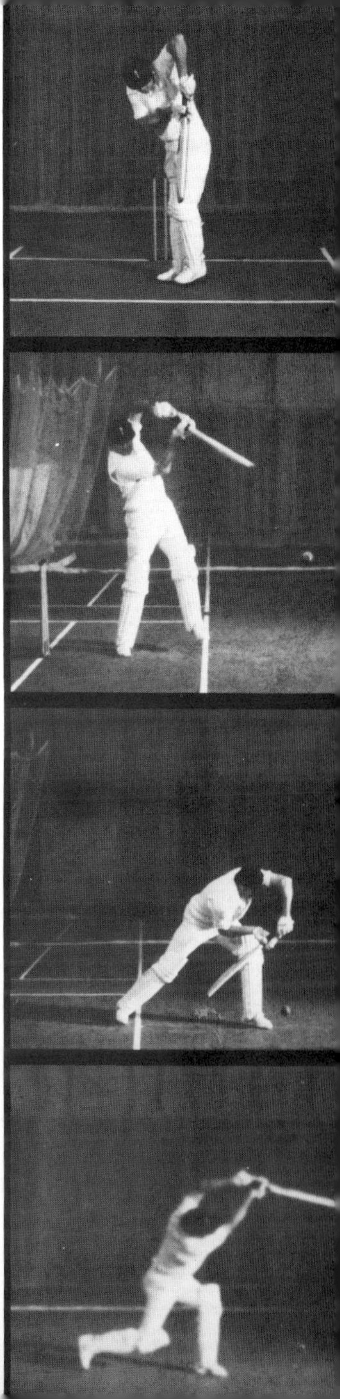

17. Cutting off the front foot

Because it is a natural cross-bat hitting shot which can be played effectively without too much technique, the cut off the front foot is popular with young players and probably provides their best chance of hitting fours.

More accomplished players do not use the stroke often because there are more sophisticated alternatives. But for youngsters who lack the strength to play the square cut powerfully – and certainly to play the forcing shot off the back foot – it is a very useful stroke.

The execution is natural and simple enough. Given a short delivery outside the off stump, the batsman puts his left foot well forward with the weight on the left leg and throws the bat down and out at the ball with arms at full stretch (Photos 37 and 38). He should contact the ball at the top of its rise and roll his wrists over to keep the ball down.

As I have said, the stroke is not favoured too much by top batsmen but it is effective and you will occasionally

England's David Gower, on to the front-foot, yet comfortably balanced to play this delivery through the off-side with a horizontal bat.

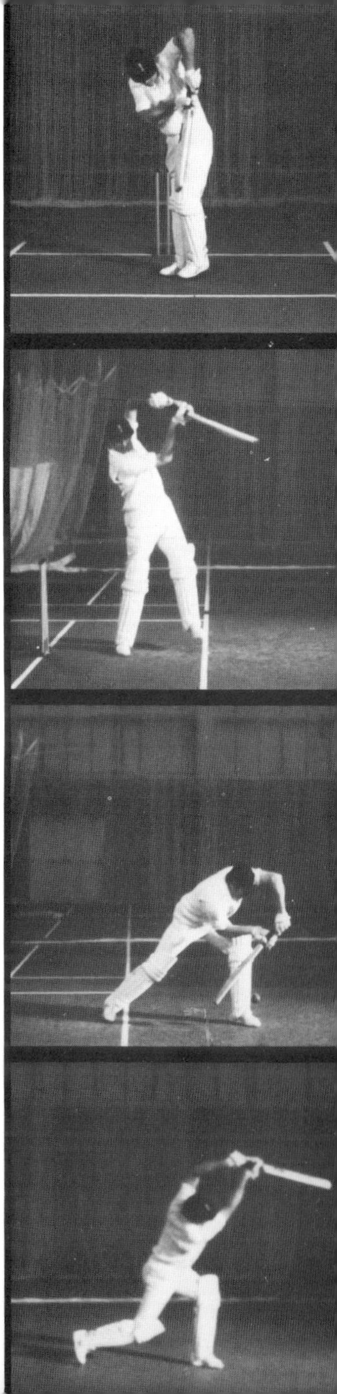

see it played in county cricket. Lower-order batsmen who tend to play practically everything off the front foot sometimes find they have miscalculated when

37

38

a delivery is short and simply use the stroke as an improvisation. It usually works, too.

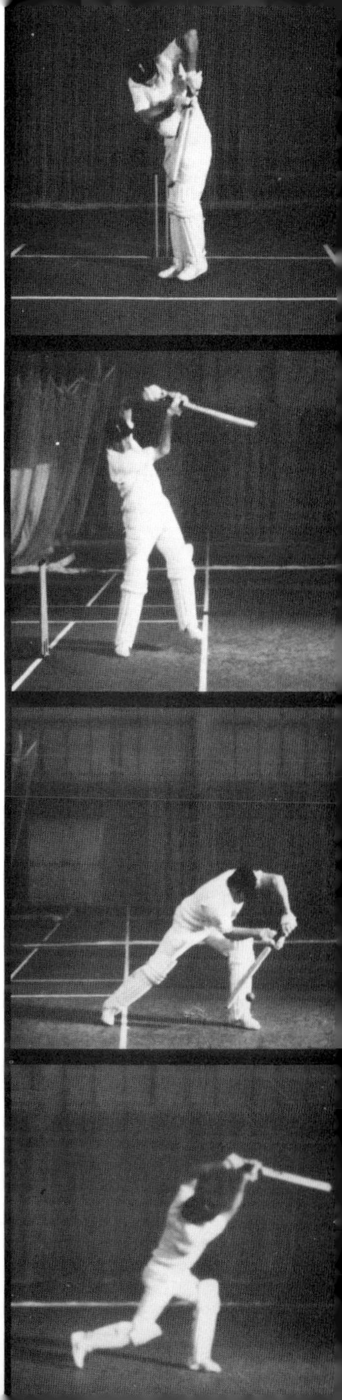

18. The lofted drive

Most batsmen who try to hit over the top seem to imagine they have to land the ball in the next field. They are so anxious to hit the ball for six (or is it twelve?) that they scoop the ball with all their might and lift their head to see how far it has gone. More often than not, it goes straight down a fielder's throat.

The lofted drive is a perfectly legitimate shot provided it is played selectively and with some tactical purpose. It might look a bit like slogging but provided it is used occasionally and sensibly it is a very useful part of a batsman's armoury, a good tactical weapon for disrupting a spinner's field placings, for example.

Strike the ball firmly rather than violently with your head down and your eye on the ball; flow down and through the ball without checking your shot and let your arms, not your body, lift the ball over the fielders. By the time you lift your head the ball should be well on its way to the boundary.

A shot Ian Botham always relishes – foot down the pitch and a full, vigorous follow-through as the ball is lofted straight back over the bowler's head.

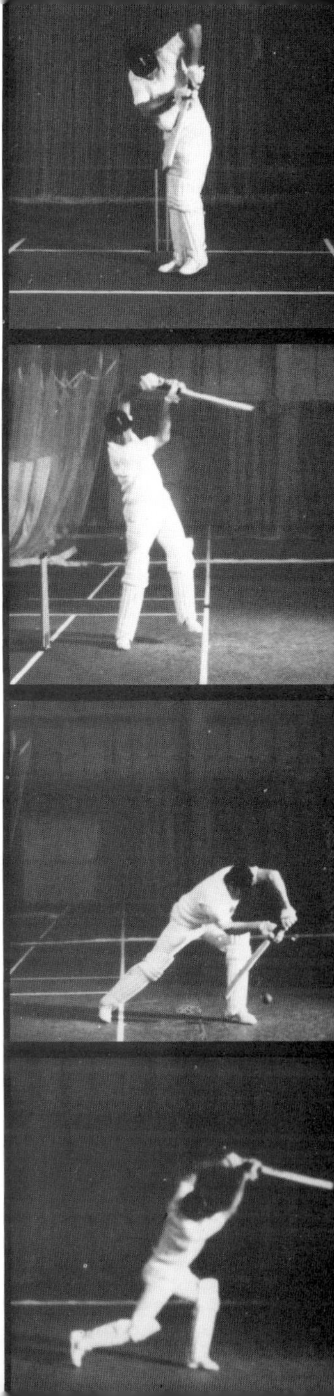

19. Equipment

Any young player keen to take up cricket naturally wants to provide himself with the best possible equipment. Just what is best for the individual is difficult to define, but there are pitfalls which can be avoided.

Choosing the right bat is vitally important. It is tempting to plump for the best-looking bat, the one which is beautifully white or has the straightest grain. Let me say right away that the appearance of the bat has absolutely nothing to do with its quality.

Select a bat for its 'feel' in the hands. That is an indefinable, personal thing because a bat is very much a matter of personal preference. But when you buy a bat, pick up several and handle them as though you were playing shots in the middle. Does it feel heavy? light? well balanced? Play a few air shots and judge the feel of the bat in your hands; select the one which picks up well and feels comfortable. A bat should not feel like a piece of wood; it should be an extension of the left arm.

Nobody can select a bat for anybody else. So if father wants to buy his boy a bat as a present he should take the lad along and let him choose the one which suits. All father can do – apart from paying, of course – is to impress on a youngster that there is no point whatsoever in buying a bat which is too big. There is no such thing as 'growing into' a good cricket bat.

Bats can be expensive, so if it is essential to save money then buy a small one rather than a big one. Even in Test cricket Sir Leonard Hutton used a Harrow-sized bat, which is at least an inch smaller than standard, and he didn't seem to suffer too much for it. . . .

There is a fashion these days for using heavy bats. That may suit the individual, especially if he is tall and strong, but I would not recommend it as a rule. A heavy bat, like a heavy driver in golf, can produce spectacular results if it is used properly, but it is difficult to control – and without control it is impossible to time the ball correctly. The aim in cricket should not be to hit one shot in four impressively but to hit every shot with timing and precision. A heavy bat will not, in itself, make you a better batsman; in fact it can have quite the opposite effect.

I use a relatively lightweight bat of

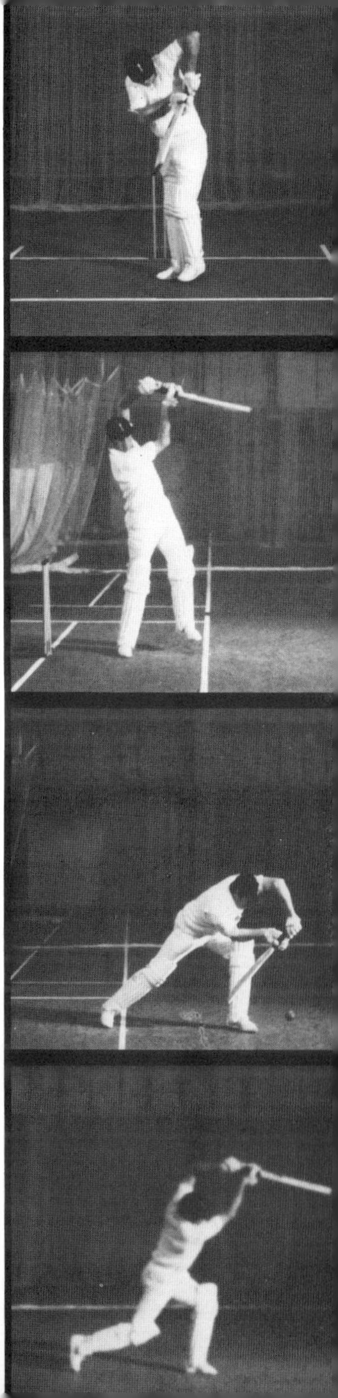

2 pounds 6 ounces, and my advice to most batsmen is to go for a lighter bat and the extra control that it gives, rather than a heavy, unmanageable one.

The length of the handle is important, and there is no earthly reason why a player of average size should use a long-handled bat. The notion that it will increase hitting power is a fallacy perhaps encouraged by cricket phrases like 'using the long handle' to mean hitting forcefully and powerfully. The only players who logically need to use a long-handled bat are tall ones: it prevents them having to stoop in the stance.

One very important point often overlooked by club cricketers is to take care of the rubber grip on the handle. So often, as grips are allowed to become smooth and shiny, so the bat slips and swivels in the hand, perhaps without the batsman being aware of it. Change the grip, with the help of some strong glue, as soon as it shows signs of slipping in the hands. Few club cricketers do and I shudder to think how many runs it costs them over a season.

Four items of equipment I consider essential to batsmen of any age are gloves, pads, a thigh pad and a protector. Always wear them when batting in a match and don't forget them in the nets or during any serious batting practice.

You may be surprised that I have included a thigh pad, which is, I suppose, a relatively modern innovation and which might not seem necessary for youngsters who do not face the very fastest bowling. But the point is that a thigh pad, like a protector, is invaluable for the sense of confidence which it gives. A cricket ball is a hard and painful object if you are at the receiving end and the proper equipment can prevent a bad bruise or a more serious injury.

It is also important to become accustomed to wearing fairly cumbersome equipment as early as possible. It is not natural to run in pads or a protector – you don't see them a lot in the Olympics! – and a thigh pad obviously adds to the general strangeness. But they are all vital pieces of protective equipment as a batsman progresses to higher grades of cricket; the sooner he learns to wear them without feeling any sense of discomfort, the better.

Perhaps the young club cricketer who wears a thigh pad will be accused of being pretentious or cissy. I think he has a lot more sense than those who

imagine it is brave or manly to risk injury.

That leads us on, inevitably these days, to the question of batting helmets. Should a young player automatically take to a helmet as he would take to a pair of batting gloves? I think not, if only because helmets are not designed for young players and they may find them *too* cumbersome and awkward. But it is a personal choice. If any player feels he needs a helmet for confidence he is entitled to wear one – so long as it genuinely helps his game and he is not just meaninglessly following a trend.

I suppose some people once laughed at players who wore batting gloves, and later pads. No doubt such players were regarded as signs of softness or lacking courage. But cricket equipment, like the game itself, is developing all the time; there is nothing cissy in accepting the confidence which proper protective equipment gives.

Many modern players favour crêpe- or rubber-soled boots – there are any number of different patterns – and they are perfectly acceptable for batting provided the pitch is hard and dry. If it is grassy or damp, metal-studded footwear is a must – and take care to keep the studs in good condition and replace them when necessary.

One final thought on equipment: keep it clean. It may be fanciful but I think the player who looks well turned out feels better and more confident; a slovenly cricketer is a dreadful sight. Some players consider a dirty bat is lucky. If they get a big score they leave the marks on the blade as though these will act as some sort of lucky talisman in the next innings. Forget it. Clean your bat after every innings with sandpaper, or wipe it with a damp cloth if it is one of the plastic-coated type.

20. Practice

Proper practice is vitally important. When young players tell me they find practice boring I suspect it's because they waste their time without any clear objective in mind. Think about practice; don't just go into the nets and slog or fool around. If you find a particular shot difficult, ask the net bowlers to bowl at you in such a way that you can practise it. And don't use more than three net bowlers if you can help it, otherwise you face a battery of deliveries without enough time between each to think about what you are doing. Using three bowlers means that you have time to think, as you would in a match, and they have time to work out what they intend to bowl; batsman and bowlers benefit.

If you find you have to practise alone, one of the very best exercises is to bat using only the left hand and arm (Photos 39 and 40). Drop the ball from your right hand and hit it into a practice net on the first bounce, gripping the bat

39

40

handle tightly with the left hand at the moment of impact. Follow through the ball with the left arm so that you finish with the arm fully extended. It really is a first-class way to improve the strength in the left arm and wrist, vitally important to any good batsman.

One important point about practice is that you should enjoy it. Don't let it become a bore or a chore because it will do very little good; better to practise often for short spells than to hammer away for long periods without feeling like it.

21. When you go in to bat

Every batsman feels nervous before he actually goes to the wicket; it's a perfectly natural thing and the nervous tension probably helps to produce that edge in performance which is so important. But some players are so nervous that they fidget and chatter in the dressing-room and don't actually watch the match in progress; that is a bad mistake.

The ability to relax before an innings can make a world of difference to playing well or badly; it is part of the temperament which becomes so important at the crease. One of the best men-in-waiting I ever met on the top-class circuit was Basil d'Oliveira; he has a marvellously bland attitude before going in to bat.

When you are waiting to bat, watch the game. That helps accustom your eyes to the light and can obviously give you a head start in judging the pace and nature of the bowling.

But don't stare fixedly at the game to

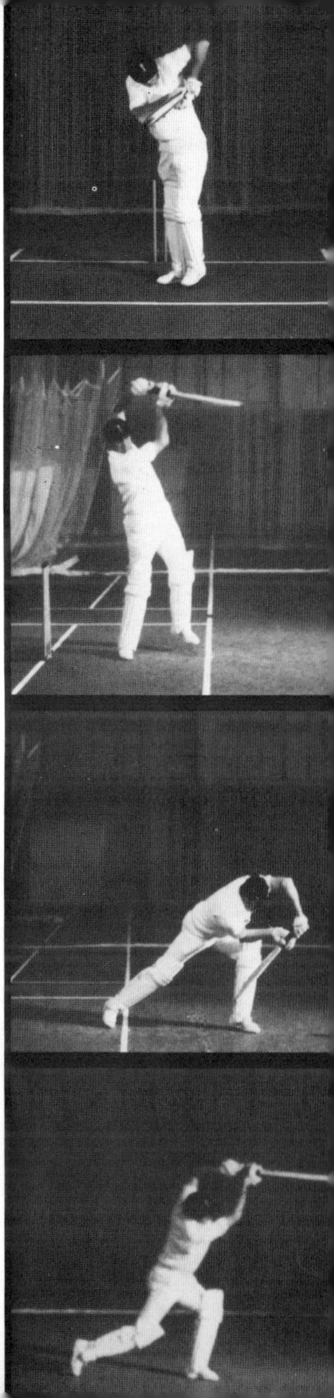

the point where you put pressure on yourself. Make a conscious effort to relax and, most important, try to stay as loose as possible. Get up and stretch your legs from time to time, bend your back and flex your shoulders. I always swing my arms from the shoulder and try to loosen my knees as I'm walking to the wicket, while Derek Randall practically dances out. It may look odd, and people may think Derek skips and jogs simply because he's nervous, but the fact is that he is taking a last opportunity to get himself loose. His antics have a purpose and a lot of merit.

If you arrive at the wicket mentally relaxed and physically loose you are in a state of readiness for the most testing part of your innings – the first few overs. Every batsman likes to get off the mark as quickly as possible but some come to grief simply because they try to play too many shots too early in their innings.

You must play yourself in, taking time to get used to the light, the bowling and the atmosphere in the middle, before you think in terms of using all your attacking strokes. Always hit the bad ball – a half volley is a half volley no matter how long you have been in – but be selective and don't expect to be striking fours from the start. Singles will build your score and your confidence just as effectively.

If you have been out of form you will feel it most strongly at the start of your innings. My advice in that situation is to cut out any fancy shots, use a straight bat and play in the *V* between mid-on and mid-off. It's a safety-first approach but if it is temporarily forced upon you, accept it and battle through.

Any bowler who is thinking about his job is going to make life especially difficult for the new batsman. So expect a quick bowler to try that bit harder and watch for the bouncer and the yorker. Anticipating a bowler's tactics is half the battle early in your innings; you must not let him outwit you. Think hard about what you are doing. Concentrate.

If the bowling is quick, employ a shorter backlift than usual and pick up the bat early. That gives you a bit of extra time to play the shot.

A good bouncer is a difficult delivery to counter but early in your innings at least, you will be content to avoid contact rather than attempt a pull or hook. Whether you duck or sway out of the line of the ball depends on whether it is aimed down the leg side, straight at the body or down the off-side. In any case,

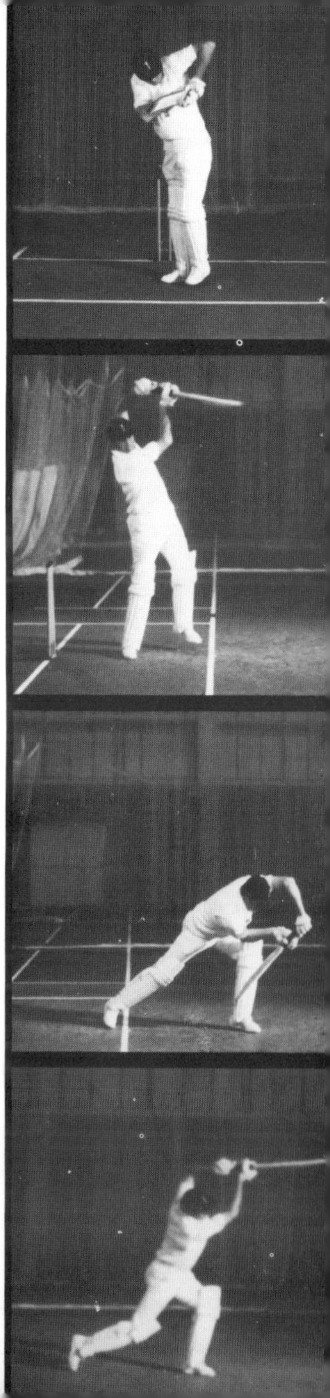

keep your eye on the ball and don't panic.

For a leg-side or straight bouncer, duck inside the ball but turn your head to watch it over the left shoulder (Photo 41); for an off-stump bouncer simply stand up straight and step or sway back to let the ball whizz harmlessly past (Photo 42).

41

42

A favourite ploy of a thinking bowler against a new batsman is to dig in a couple of short deliveries to force him on to the back foot and then pitch the next delivery well up to beat him or get an l.b.w. decision. Be aware of the possibility. Think about it.

Many incoming batsmen have a quick look round the field without really forming a mental picture of where

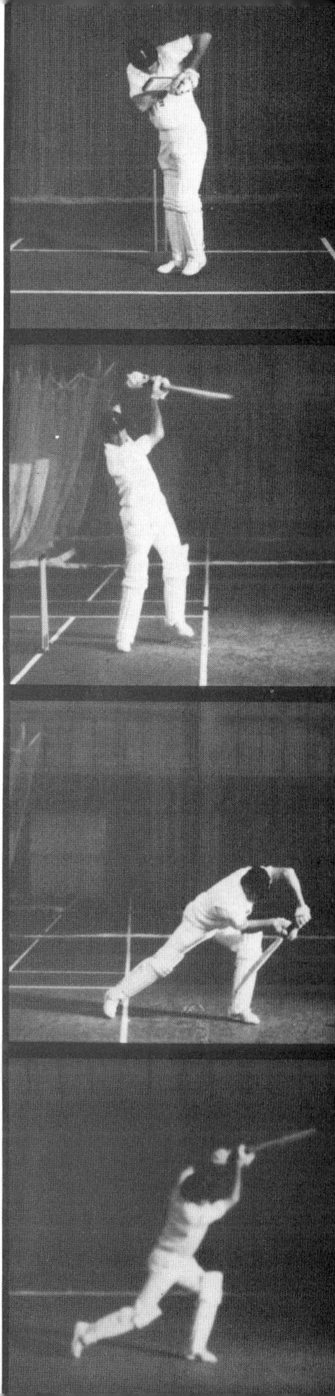

fielders are placed. That is a mistake: unless you know just where the fielders are, you cannot possibly spot the gaps.

Even if you have been watching closely before actually going in, the chances are that the bowler will change his field for the new batsman so it's essential to check. Don't take anything for granted; re-check the field placings at least once an over even if you don't think there have been any changes.

Finally, the English summer being what it is, the chances are that you will often have to play in wet or windy conditions. As a rule, it is fatal to attempt to drive off the front foot on a wet pitch because the soggy turf makes the ball stop and you are likely to spoon catches. Play back whenever possible and let the ball come on to you; that way you have more time to play your shot and are well positioned to cut, hook or pull if the ball really stands up. Windy conditions disturb a batsman's balance and make it very difficult to control the bat. The best counter is to shorten your backlift and then punch the ball with a shortened follow-through; that helps to keep your balance and preserves your timing.

There is an old saying that you get as much out of the game of cricket as you put into it. Just how hard and long you are prepared to practise is up to you, but there is a tremendous amount of pleasure to be gained not just from playing the game but from the knowledge that you play it properly and well.

I hope this book will help you master the basic techniques of batting and provide a reference which you can go back to when things don't seem to be going right. Work at your practice, work at your game and above all enjoy both – there really is no game in the world like it. Good luck.

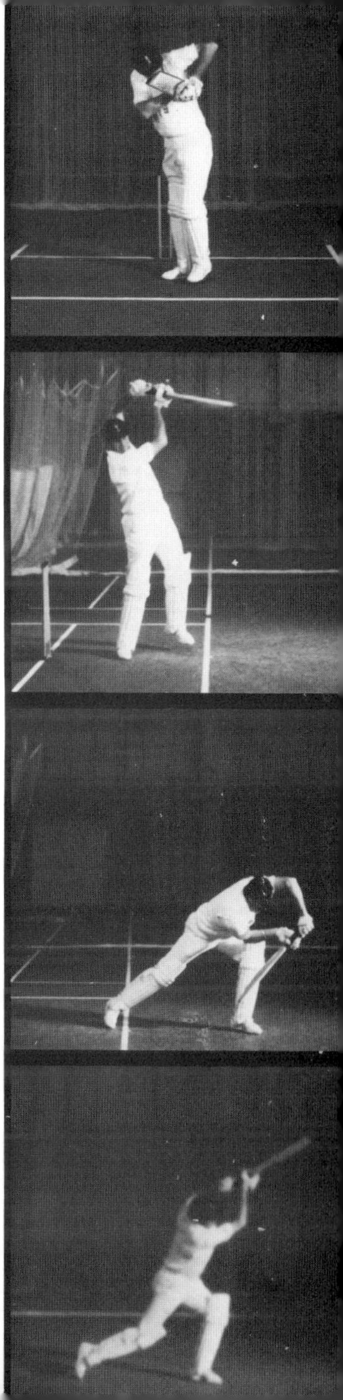

A selection of world-class batsmen

One of India's little masters – Gundappa Viswanath. Here, he is in perfect position to pull a short ball through mid-wicket during the Lord's Test of 1979.

Typical Clive Lloyd – on to the front foot, his weight balanced as the ball is punched through mid-wicket.

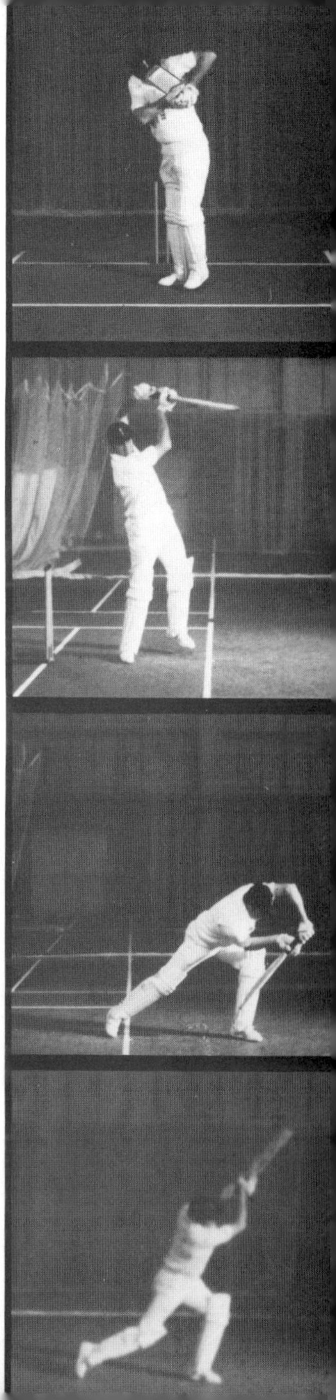

Asif Iqbal looking, as ever, full of enthusiasm as he goes down on one knee in the classic pose for sweeping the off-spinner.

A player of delicate touch, delightful timing, Pakistan's Zaheer Abbas glides this delivery behind square-leg, virtually on the run.

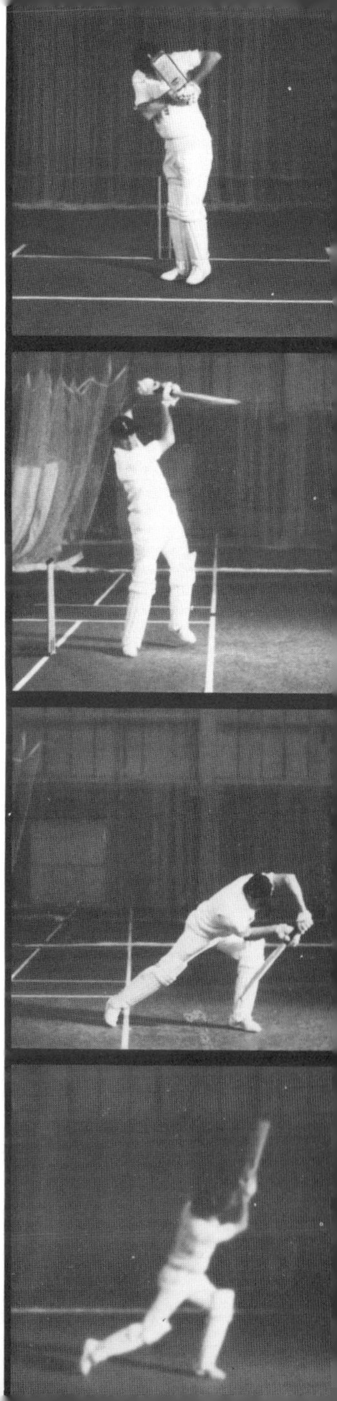

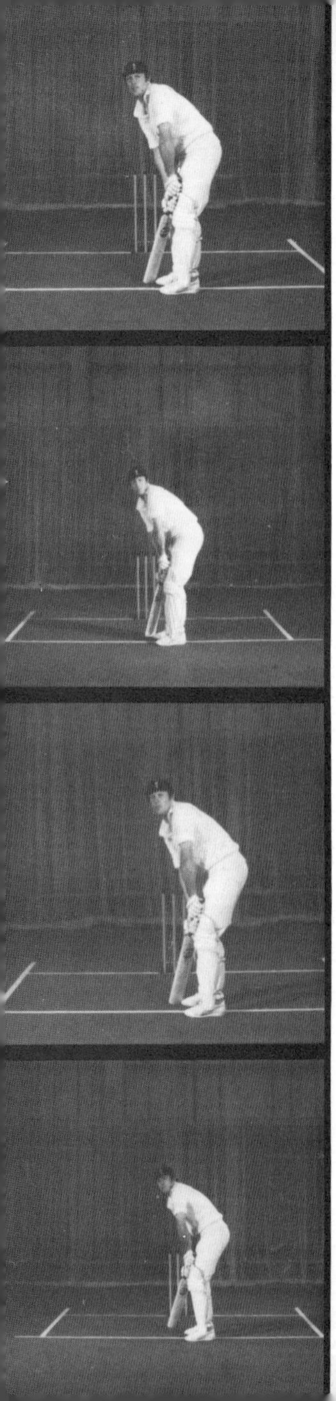

Glenn Turner, of Worcestershire and New Zealand, demonstrating the art of the cover drive. The front foot is firmly but comfortably forward, the eyes down to follow the ball.

England's Graham Gooch, balancing on the toes of each foot, drives firmly and confidently through mid-off during his century in the 1979 Benson and Hedges Cup Final.

Playing Back Defensively

The On Drive

The Late Cut

The Off Drive

Mike Procter, Gloucestershire's South African captain and all-rounder supreme, moving out to drive elegantly through the cover region.

Barry Richards literally rocking on to the back foot to hook, yet controlling the shot expertly by rolling his right wrist to keep the ball down.